Wild Anima[ls]

RACCOONS

GAIL TERP

Black Rabbit Books

Bolt is published by Black Rabbit Books
P.O. Box 3263, Mankato, Minnesota, 56002.
www.blackrabbitbooks.com
Copyright © 2017 Black Rabbit Books

Design and Production by Michael Sellner
Photo Research by Rhonda Milbrett

All rights reserved. No part of this book may be reproduced in any form without written permission from the publisher.

Library of Congress Control Number: 2015954867

HC ISBN: 978-1-68072-055-6   PB ISBN: 978-1-68072-312-0

Printed in the United States at CG Book Printers, North Mankato, Minnesota, 56003. PO #1798 4/16

Web addresses included in this book were working and appropriate at the time of publication. The publisher is not responsible for broken or changed links.

Image Credits

Alamy: Rolf Nussbaumer, 22; Biosphoto: Fabien Bruggmann, 21 (top); Nat Geo: TIM FITZHARRIS, 28 (full page); Photoshot: Nick Hawkins, 14 (full page); Science Source: Steve Maslowski, 11; Shutterstock: andamanec, Cover; Andrey Pavlov, 27 (ants); Becky Sheridan, 4–5, 28 (bottom); Bildagentur Zoonar GmbH, 8; dangdumrong, 3, 32; David Unger, 21 (bottom); Dionisvera, 27 (acorns); editha, 19 (bottom); Eric Isselee, 6–7, 27 (raccoon and mouse); Gala Che, 23 (right); Gerald A. DeBoer, 19 (top); IrinaK, 18 (right); Jean-Edouard Rozey, 27 (coyote); jennyt, Back Cover, 1, 17; JIANG HONGYAN, 27 (corn); PhotoHouse, 12, 23 (silhouette); Robert Eastman, 27 (bobcat); Svet-lana, 18 (left); Svetlana Foote, 31; tjwvandongen, 14 (bottom); Tony Campbell, 24–25; Ultrashock, 8–9; Victoria Novak, 12 (background)

Every effort has been made to contact copyright holders for material reproduced in this book. Any omissions will be rectified in subsequent printings if notice is given to the publisher.

Contents

CHAPTER 1
A Day in the Life 4

CHAPTER 2
Food to Eat and
a Place to Live 10

CHAPTER 3
Family Life 20

CHAPTER 4
Predators and
Other Threats. 24

Other Resources. 30

CHAPTER 1

A Day in the Life

A raccoon moves quickly through the trees. With its gray fur, it blends right into the dark woods. Finding its way in the low light is easy. A raccoon's night **vision** is very good. Its hearing is good too.

The raccoon comes to an old log. It uses its sharp claws to tear the log apart. Long front toes grab the hiding bugs. They are a great meal for a raccoon.

RACCOON FEATURES

BLACK MASK AROUND EYES

LONG, FLUFFY TAIL WITH RINGS

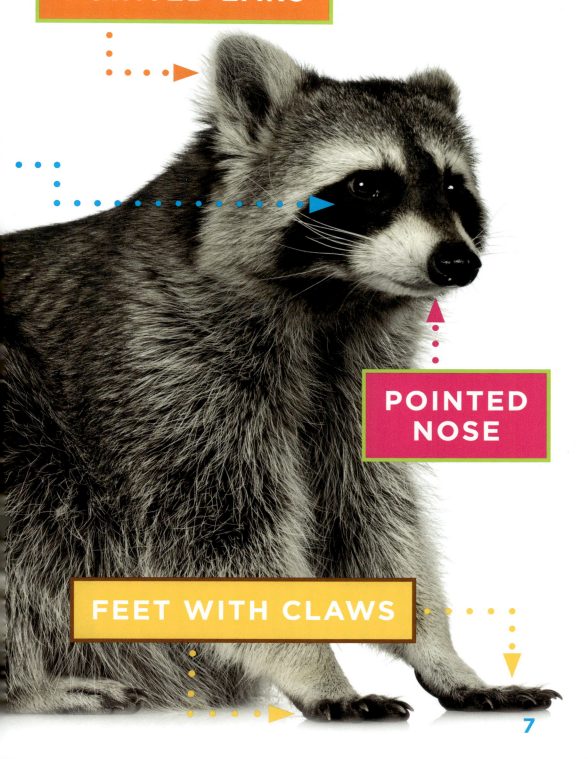

WEIGHT
14 TO 23 POUNDS
(6 TO 10 KILOGRAMS)

Acorn Feast

Next, the raccoon climbs a tree with acorns. It gobbles as many as it can. Its body stores the extra food as fat. The fat will help the animal survive winter.

How Big Is a Raccoon?

**LENGTH
24 TO 38 INCHES
(61 to 97 centimeters)**

CHAPTER 2

Food to Eat
and a Place to Live

Raccoons live in a wide range of **habitats**. They are often found in woods and swamps. They sleep during the day in **dens**. A den could be in a **hollow** tree. It might be in a crack between rocks.

Raccoons eat a wide range of foods. For plants, they eat nuts and fruits. For meat, they go after insects, mice, and birds. Raccoons eat garbage too.

WHERE RACCOONS LIVE

Raccoon Range Map

Night Hunters

Raccoons are **nocturnal** hunters. They use their front paws to find food. Their paws have five long toes. The toes have a great sense of touch. Their sense of touch is so good, they can find food underwater. They don't even have to look.

Not Food Washers

Raccoons often dunk their food in water. They're not washing it. Water helps raccoons feel their food.

City Raccoons

Many raccoons live in cities. Cities have food, such as garbage and pet food, that's been left out. Basements, crawl spaces, or chimneys make great homes.

A raccoon paw print is easy to spot. It looks a lot like a human handprint.

By the Numbers

2 to 3 YEARS — AVERAGE LIFE SPAN

8 TO 10 INCHES (20 TO 25 CM) — AVERAGE TAIL LENGTH

40 TEETH

1 TO 9
NUMBER OF CUBS BORN AT ONE TIME

2.3 OUNCES (65 GRAMS)
AVERAGE BIRTH WEIGHT

15 MILES (24 KILOMETERS) PER HOUR
TOP RUNNING SPEED

CHAPTER 3

In spring, females make dens in hollow trees. They give birth to up to nine cubs. Cubs are born with their eyes closed. At three weeks, they open their eyes.

Down the Tree

Raccoons can climb down trees head first. They turn their feet to grip the bark.

COMPARING SIZES

Growing Up

Cubs start to hunt with their mothers when they are two or three months old. They stay with their mothers through the winter. In spring, most leave to live on their own.

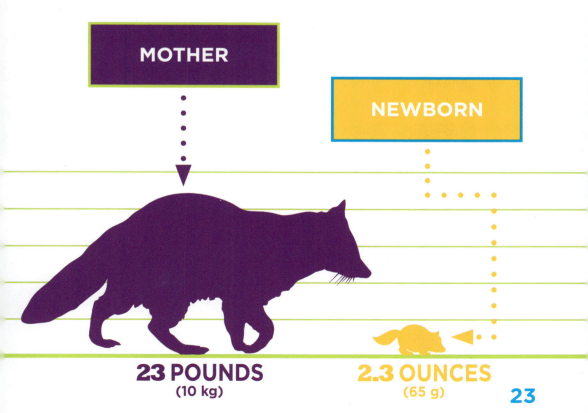

MOTHER
NEWBORN
23 POUNDS (10 kg)
2.3 OUNCES (65 g)

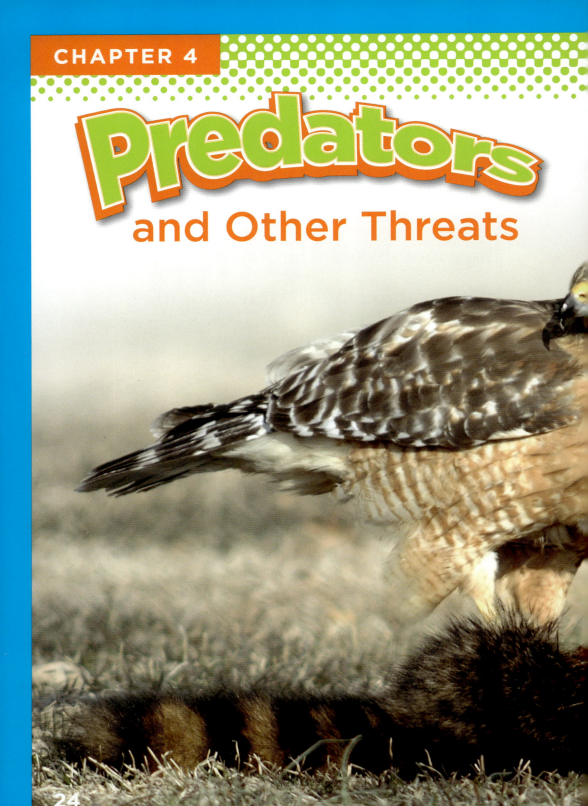

CHAPTER 4

Predators
and Other Threats

Coyotes and bobcats are **predators** of raccoons. Hawks and snakes are too. Humans are also a **threat**. They hunt and trap raccoons. Cars sometimes hit raccoons as the animals cross roads.

Farm Trouble

Raccoons can cause problems on farms. They eat corn and other crops. They kill chickens. Some farmers hunt or trap raccoons to protect their farms.

Raccoon Food Chain

This **food chain** shows what eats raccoons. It also shows what raccoons eat.

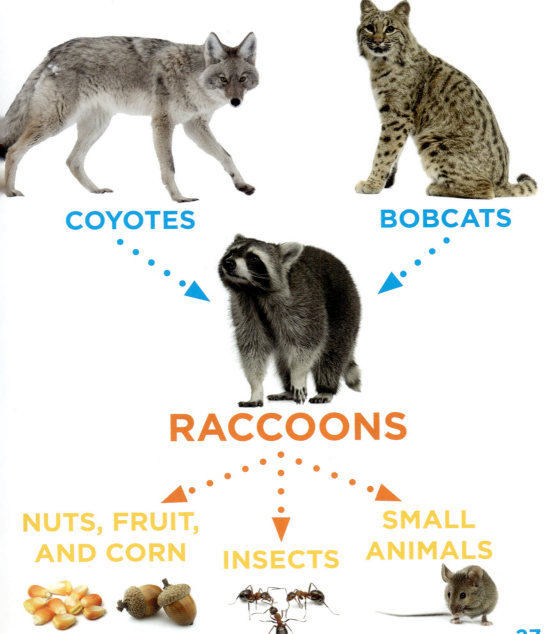

Raccoons Adapt

Raccoons live in woods and swamps. They also live in the country and in towns. And they find food wherever they go. Raccoons are pros at fitting in!

Raccoons will eat any food left out, including vegetables, garbage, and pet food.

GLOSSARY

den (DEN)—the home of some kinds of wild animals

food chain (FOOD CHAYN)—a series of plants and animals in which each uses the next in the series as a food source

habitat (HAB-uh-tat)—the place where a plant or animal grows or lives

hollow (HAWL-oh)—an unfilled space

nocturnal (NOK-turn-uhl)—active at night

predator (PRED-uh-tuhr)—an animal that eats other animals

threat (THRET)—something that can do harm

vision (VI-zhun)—eyesight

LEARN MORE

BOOKS

Bowman, Chris. *Raccoons*. North American Animals. Minneapolis: Bellwether Media, Inc., 2016.

Gish, Melissa. *Raccoons*. Living Wild. Mankato, MN: Creative Education, 2015.

Scott, Traer. *Nocturne: Creatures of the Night*. New York: Princeton Architectural Press, 2014.

WEBSITES

North American Raccoon
kids.sandiegozoo.org/animals/mammals/north-american-raccoon

Raccoon
kids.nationalgeographic.com/animals/raccoon/

Raccoon
www.biokids.umich.edu/critters/Procyon_lotor/

INDEX

C
cubs, 19, 20, 23

F
features, 4, 6–7, 15, 18, 21

food, 4, 9, 10, 15, 16, 27, 29

H
habitats, 10, 16, 29

P
predators, 25, 27

R
ranges, 12–13

S
sizes, 8–9, 18–19, 23

speeds, 19